Jack
by Mike Spry

Jack
by Mike Spry

Snare Books . Montreal . 2008

Copyright © 2008 by Mike Spry
All rights reserved. No part of this publication may be reproduced, stored in a retrieval system or transmitted, in any form or by any means without the prior written permission of the publisher.

Edited by David McGimpsey
Designed by Jon Paul Fiorentino
Copyedited by Marisa Grizenko
Typeset in Gill Sans and Adobe Garamond

Library and Archives Canada Cataloguing in Publication

Spry, Mike, 1976-
　　Jack / Mike Spry.

Poems.
ISBN 978-0-9739438-7-0

　　I. Title.

PS8637.P79J32 2008　　　　C811'.6　　　C2008-904787-7

Printed and bound in Canada
Represented in Canada by the Literary Press Group
Distributed by LitDistCo

SNARE BOOKS
4832 A Avenue Du Parc
Montreal QC
H2V 4E6
snarebooks.wordpress.com

Snare Books gratefully acknowledges the financial support of the Canada Council for the Arts.

 **Canada Council　Conseil des Arts
for the Arts　　du Canada**

for Hillary

Contents

I. Loose Corn Daiquiris
II. Battery Milk
III. Convenience

jack.
    (1) The diminutive of *John*. Used as a general term of contempt for saucy or paltry fellows.
    (2) The name of instruments which supply the place of a boy, as an instrument to pull off boots.
    (3) An engine that turns the spit.
    (6) A cup of waxed leather.
Dead wine, that stinks of the borrachio, sup. From a foul *jack*, or greasy mapple cup. Dryden's *Persius*.

I. Loose Corn Daiquiris

Idleness Foxglove

ANON.
Nights drinking kerosene
with strays in Ottawa dog parks,
nervously lighting cigarettes,
humming Neil Young songs

that strummed fond thoughts,
hoping one day we'd turn eighteen,
then one day wishing
we could turn back.

Instead it rained cell phone leashes and bleeding ulcers.
Soon we'd become inhospitable garden party hosts
selling opinions soaked in rye
to happily married adulterers.

I was sharing a king can of 50 with a dishevelled mutt,
and just like that I was thirty.

JACK
Jack is not my friend. Jack is my friend.
I do not like Jack. I will not know Jack.
Jack is successful. Jack is a vegetarian in leper skin boots.
Jack will quote scripture while fucking your wife.

And the roof of thy mouth
like the best wine for my beloved,
that goeth down sweetly,
causing the lips of those that are asleep to speak.

Jack will eat your soul and then tell you it's over-salted.
Jack keeps his bible in a Ziploc bag,
takes it out to settle arguments and draw straight lines.
Jack drinks Jack and Coke so that he can refer to his drink

in the third person. "Do us a favour and top up Jack
for Jack. Don't forget Jack's cubes." Jack is married to Ruth.

RUTH
Ruth is indeed Jack's wife. Ruth is Jack's mother.
Ruth collects pictures of other people's children.
Ruth has dinner ready every day at six-thirty.
Ruth has her mother's hips and tuna casserole recipe.

Ruth thinks Ray Romano is a hoot.
Ruth has never had an orgasm.
Ruth has never pulled at Jack's hair
and cried his name as she came.

Ruth is a vacant smiling sadness. Compliments
feel like indictments of yesterday. The wallpaper
in the washroom is very pretty, it reminds her
of her mother's funeral. Ruth has many prescriptions:

Fluoxetine, Olanzapine, selected Niagara
Peninsula Chardonnays, and unaffectionate vibrators.

DAVE
Dave comes alone with his guitar.
Dave once prayed to be a rock star.
Dave is bitter that he isn't.
Dave believes God owed him that,

because he could play three chords.
She ain't nice like my mother, and she hits like my father,
and while I still miss her kiss, she's still addicted to bein' a bitch.
Dave smiles while chewing his teeth in a quiet contempt for you.

Dave has his addictions written on the back of *Jitterbug Perfume*,
next to his first love's last phone number. Dave lives in 1992.

Dave sings sad slow suffocating songs about impotence and
hockey and God. Dave masturbates to images of dead flowers.

Do you mind if I take a picture of those wilting dahlias?
This room is vicious, like a woman, like a flower.

JANE
Jane is married to the unshaven vagrant in my mirror.
Jane keeps her rage in a jar underneath the sink,
brings it out at parties to impress our friends.
Jane wishes she played piano.

Jane uses the word divorce very casually.
Jane gives disinterested head.
Sometimes, when I'm not around,
Jane likes the third person and scripture.

I think Jane killed another Jane. A younger Jane. My Jane.
Jane keeps her love for me in the bottom of a bottle of Stolly.
In angry whispers Jane says I won't father her children.
Jane doesn't know I'm sterile. Jane doesn't appreciate irony.

What about last night?
Don't confuse acquittal with passion.

ANON.
I am untitled. I am anonymous.
I have become sullen and bitter.
I understand light beer and sulking.
I keep a stale pack of Peter Jacksons hidden in my garage.

I lie about unimportant details of an inconsequential life
for unapparent reasons, like the colour of my Hyundai
or the age of my dog. I don't own a dog.
I am constantly recalculating my existence on cocktail napkins.

These walls will fold and sway as I dance my *Old Man*'s waltz
hoping to reclaim those kerosene nights
with strays in Ottawa dog parks,
nervously lighting cigarettes,

humming Neil Young songs, strumming fond thoughts
that one day we could turn back and be eighteen again.

Ampersand

I.
& you sit alone in rooms reeking of sulphur & arrogance
as children in their twenties argue the merits of Marlowe,
Samuel Richardson & Chuck Norris.

& you know tonight each child will drink enough confidence
to go home disappointed, naive to the knowledge
that nights last longer than hangovers,

longer than Nana's last scotch,
longer than *Doctor Faustus* or *Pamela*,
longer than the *Missing in Action* trilogy.

& everyday is like the day you found out a dandelion
is not a flower or your lover didn't care how you felt,
when you realised she was everybody else.

& everyday lives in Starbucks' premium-blend culture,
while your peers, who left you behind long ago,
discuss Volkswagens, ecru lies, one night stands

& dishwasher safe Hungarian vibrators.
& you think maybe, just maybe, if someone loved you,
or if you had a Jetta, you just might be okay.

& your nights, alone, in the corners of mail-order Irish pubs,
wondering how many forests have died in the name of coasters,
the number of marriages spawned by vending machine condoms,
& why the last pint no longer makes you smile.

II.
& currently on your coffee table: dinner from last Tuesday,
a doodle of what is either a crippled mallard
        or a Thai hooker missing an eye,
three cigarettes, a remote control for a stereo you no longer own,

an unread copy of *One Hundred Years of Solitude*, a match pack
with six sevenths of what may be an important phone number,
a fading photograph of life's lumbering gait,

a losing lottery ticket from nineteen ninety-seven,
an empty pack of extra strength mint Rolaids,
your one source of calcium, believing milk like Mondays,
        to be full of lies.

III.
& you find yourself in places you never imagined,
like suburban Ontario, like in a bathtub of burgundy with Jesus,
singing Supertramp & worrying about the Lord's falsetto.

like in the arms of broken women,
who are comforted in being left wanting,
for love & faith & bus fare.

IV.
Ten years later & you still hate decades,
couples & carrots, European sedans,
Saturday mornings & operatic ballad rock.

& you sit in a room where you're the king,
of four walls, both monarch & fool,
but unwilling to choose.

ten years from now the kingdom survives, its walls decorated
in some other memories, the light comes & goes
for stranger's eyes, the gloaming keeping someone else company.

A quiet palace in the absence of a queen, a museum of context,
awaits a guest that comes & goes for the last time,
a room full of doors, & not a goddamn shelf.

V.
But fucking carrots, with their contemptuous orange glow,
their perfectly confident rigidity, mistress of the optician,
the smug dangled root.

& nobody ever says: "he was hung like a carrot,"
"hard as a carrot" or "kind & selfless as a carrot,"
but they're thinking it.

& the carrot's homonymous cousin, the karat, whose absence
keeps you single. Unless you find one opulent enough,
splattered the blood of a thousand & five South Africans,

than you will die alone, in a room, a room full of her.
& you'll be wondering if it gets any better,
because you know (you know) for her, it does.

Jane (Mount Royal)

And you with your smile.
And you with your smile.

And gin laced sentiment
of moving up to the Mile End,
rugged and earnest
as the mountain's inclined.

This is the sun drunk afternoon
and three perfect ice cubes,
in a city where west is north,
where October's foliage teases

like the caramel kindness
of barrel smoked whiskies.
And our only fears are
right turns and separation.

Your breath a sweet subtle mixture
of tobacco, last night, and regret
bundled warmly in a defensive wit
and an ex-lover's hooded fleece.

And you with your smile.
And you with your smile.

Explaining 4:11

INT. – JANE'S APT. – 4:11AM
Jane comes home late, drunk enough not to sleep,
reads a poem about herself in which she's the star
of a foreign film that has no subtitles or plot or resolution.

But it has a sweaty bearded hero,
though the actor playing him seems too aware
of her screen presence and the film suffers for it.

What it lacks is made up for with clever camera work,
good lighting, and Jane is more beautiful than I remember
on that August day when she asked me to marry her.

INT. – ANON. APT. – 4:11AM
I used to be in a band, played alt.country indie metal swing.
All the songs were about Dave's ex-girlfriend,
not that the rest of us didn't write or have ex-girlfriends.

He seemed to breathe the experience in clumsy chords,
solos preaching brevity. His rhymes uncontrived,
his refrains haunting, like a weathered cross on a highway.

There's a picture Jane took of the band,
naked in front of a 7-Eleven in mid-March,
with toques over our genitals and 50 caps glued to our nipples.

From time to time at 4:11, I find the photo.
All I can see is my hopeless eyes on the photographer,
and Dave's erect CBC hat with a yellow pom-pom.

INT. – ANON. APT. – 4:11AM
I wake up to catch the dawn, tease it about the gloaming,
sip leftover beer, not quite dregs, not too proud.
One more, so the morning won't complain.

Wonder if maybe I should be taking more pictures
that I'll never develop, in case I soon forget
why it is that 4:11 wakes me up.

Why I make juvenile prayers on those elevens,
asking for you to come back, or a belief in God,
just so I have someone to argue with.

Why whispers of vodka dreams, too recent to be forgotten
sift through old photographs sorting memory,
planning for our future despite my lack of faith in it.

INT. – BAR – 4:11AM
When my dad died she left me for Jack.
I was angry at my dad, as if he had timed it all.
One last twisted fucking joke, childish games from soft graves.

I drank his prescription scotch, smoked his palliative duMauriers
wishing she could've waited till the eulogy's last note
to move on to a man who looks good in a suit.

Soon I'll go back to bartending,
drink long lunches, live off lonely housewives,
and build bleachers around me.

I ask for a 50. It's 4:11 somewhere.
The bartender, holding an ambered rag,
points out a girl across the room I once loved enough to leave.

We talk about my faults, she goes through them alphabetically,
from asshole to zenophobe. I'm humbled,
more so by her organizational skills than anything else.

When she goes to leave, a film's ending frames my mind,
I pull her close, her mouth within a convoluted whisper of mine.
Everything I want is there for the taking.

Instead I kissed her cheek, resolved to wallow.
Comforted in knowing I did nothing. I'll wrap myself in that,
like the half-empty bottle that warms me on cold nights,

in August memories, in long refrains, the North wind
waking at 4:11, when the bed is half-empty
and the morning promises nothing but another fucking day.

Open Source Messiahs and Terrestrial Radio

Agonize for forty-two minutes over whether solace
is a cheap bottle of vodka or a bottle of cheap vodka.

Solitude other than the fabrications of silence
and a faltering radio, now known as terrestrial radio.

Is this new title permanent? The distinction important?
Email me if you know the answer, or just to say hey.

Wonder if today's the day impotence finally arrives,
in its Coppertone smile and easy manner.

I'll test myself before I sleep. Impotence before importance,
before knowledgeable and confused nightmares anyway.

Maybe start stealing Viagra from the purses of pocket drunks
predicting tomorrows from the soft corners of bedroom bars.

Custodial drink service, repairing the interminably unserviceable,
toothless deities slurring bumper sticker wisdom

(*Cash, Grass or Ass, Nobody Rides for Free.*
Never wrestle with a pig. You get dirty and the pig enjoys it.)

arguing the merits of problem days
that have perhaps been solved in my absences.

Street preaching and cumbersome recollections,
it has all been theatre lately. Last night's drinks cleaning

aesthetics coloured by vanity. Apprehension and bad numbers,
housing repressed love, rooms of things I should have said:

I lie about my smiles. You look beautiful in my shirts.
My lovers didn't always have last names.

My watch says it's yesterday, I wonder if you're awake.
I've spent the last week awake in worry

it will never be tomorrow,
I'll never get home to empty those rooms.

Your message read: "God is a punch line. Jesus is a chain smoker
living two doors down. His cat is humourless and in heat."

The water here is cold and rusted. Neil was right,
so I'm bending forty-two days in a quiet attempt to burnout.

Marginalized by that which I cannot control,
and in these unjustified stanzas I hope we'll find

the meaning that has been missing,
in the manicured days you fear.

Eight pound favours and featherweight writers,
tainted attempts at postcard memories, better left to postscript.

Closed cupboards housing heaven heavy as church doors,
glass messiahs and picture frames turned down.

Compelled by the patterns in beaten hardwood flooring,
angry construction from a city suffering from low self-esteem.

A dial tone that is no longer comforting.
Someone else used to live here. It was me, I think.

Spend whole weeks lost in search of chorus epiphanies,
asking calming chords and familiar refrains

how it is that terrestrial radio, barstool brethren,
distance and empty bottles know me so well.

Let Us Feel Satisfied, Our 'R's Before Our 'E's

Three things I have recently learned about women,
of whom I have varied experience yet little knowledge:

One, the hymen apparently can grow back.
This fact makes me wonder if we, the circumcised,
can manage a similar regeneration.

Two, the sexually frustrated female is susceptible
to an ailment not unlike blue balls. Vasocongestion.
Had I known this as a younger man,

my high school beggings would have seemed sadder,
more petty than they already do. For this I wish to apologize
to my high school sweetheart. And to her sister.

Three, and perhaps the least surprising,
women don't like to be called Steve
or Ethan when in the throws of passion.

This morning I awoke next to a young woman,
let's call her Ethan, and Ethan says to me:
"Steve, let's go back to sleep, let's wake up somewhere else."

And I think, at least you have not woken up in Belleville, Ethan.
At least you have not woken up in Smiths Falls,
in North Bay, or anywhere in Saskatchewan.

If you woke up in one of those places.
Junior "A" hockey places, you might not know
about the amazing hymen, about blue balls, about me.

If you woke up in one of those places, idealizing Sudbury,
worshipping Toronto, wishing for Calgary, watching curling,
your name would not be Ethan. You'd be Jennifer. Or Ruby Mae.

Ruby Mae who gets all the good shifts at Timmy's.
Ruby Mae who blows right-wingers, and only right-wingers.
Ruby Mae who marries the goalie with a torn ACL.

You'd never leave home. The wedding would be at centre ice.
The reception would be at the Legion. Your hair would be awful.
You'd dance with your father to Chilliwack's "I Believe."

Your life would be most unhappy, Ethan.
So let's arise here in Montreal and fight the morning,
fight blue balls, break your magic hymen again and again.

Let's go south to Vermont for St. Jean Baptiste Day.
Let's get my car out of the garage, grab some smokes
and get out on the road.

Let's teach Montpelier, Rutland and Newport,
the Green Mountain State about hymens and vasocongestion.
Let's get a room and feel what it is like to fuck Vermont-style,

to fuck away from the Mountain's glow,
to come in America's face,
(and by America's face I mean your face),

to come on the overly starched
sheets of an east coast Best Western.
Let us fuck for all those Jennifers and Ruby Maes.

Let us fuck for all of those who never left Wawa.
Let us fuck for the couple celebrating their tenth anniversary
with quarts of 50 in the back of the Legion.

Oh Ethan, sweet hymenless undersatisfied frustrated Ethan.
Let us fuck like Canadians. Let us fuck between periods.
Let us fuck like Toronto-hating curling-addled Canadians

and hurry hard to relieve our vasocongestion.
Let us fuck below the border with extra 'u's.
Let us feel satisfied, our 'r's before our 'e's.

Calculated Distractions in the Absence of Someone Named Jane

Bless me Labatt 50, for I have sinned,
in the age of well-manicured indifference,
in the reflection of puddling beer,
in the absence of someone named Jane.

I am a Habs fan and an adulterer,
a chain smoker and a Virgo,
in a quiet decade of acquaintances
and in the absence of friends.

I consider my name and circumcision,
angered that my parents neglected to consult me,
wonder if science has yet progressed
to where surgical reversal is at all possible.

I wonder if my mother's OB/GYN ever thinks about me,
or if our nine month association was meaningless.
Whatever happened to my umbilical cord?
Does it miss me? Does it ask about me? Can it do long division?

I mull over the fact I may have worn my last condom.
Not because of a troublesome left curve, however uncomfortable.
Not because health insurance doesn't cover Viagra, or escorts.
And certainly not because of the absence of someone named Jane.

I recently cut the pockets off all of my slacks,
coloured my hair a violent shade of ruby,
became addicted to googling "blonde Filipinos",
and changed my outlook from bitter to cynical.

I have decided that in the privacy of my home,
I will listen only to Will Oldham and the Silver Jews.

Though in public I swear allegiance to Poison and Van Halen,
and argue the merits of the Gary Cherone era.

At an auction recently, I bought Brian Mulroney's barstools,
painted them a colour that can best be described as daffodil,
took them out into the backyard and lit them on fire, doused
the blaze with urine as my neighbours played backgammon.

My drink and I will, tonight, discuss the following:
The calculated confidence of fortune cookies.
Friends: clever sitcom or vehicle for self-destruction?
The poetic justice that was John Denver's death.

The misappropriation of Airbus funds.
The homogenization of contemporary pornography.
The misguided swagger of Malaysian cuisine.
Why facial hair grows while pubic hair, seemingly, does not.

The genius of Jerry Orbach, whatever happened to Swatches.
That cocksucker, the internal combustion engine, colon cancer,
the mistake that is Taco Bell, things that used to be red,
right turns, left turns, brinkmanship, and U-turns,

Whether every rose has its thorn,
Whether every night has its dawn,
Whether every cowboy sings his sad, sad song,
Whether anyone has ever had a worse Easter than Jesus?

And why I drink, in the absence of someone named Jane.

I-5

SEATTLE, WASHINGTON
The sign read: *101 Beautiful Naked Women and 3 Ugly Ones.*
Most girls wouldn't have wanted to stop,
but she had nice porno eyes,
easing the Volvo to the curb.

Inside we drank flat expensive draught,
watched single mothers dance for indie kids,
in the absence of fat businessmen sweating
small erections through Sears suits.

Pinstripe fiends on long lunches from sad cubicles
that have somehow grown like weeds in a suburbia
that stretches up and down Interstate 5.
I asked the bartender, whose nametag said Horatio

(but his eyes, his eyes said Fortinbras),
where the "Ugly Ones" were.
Horatio said they weren't so much ugly as bitter
at a world painted in suburban strip club teal.

She was an actress, or a waitress.
Not sure if I know the difference.
I wrote her introspective post-modern performance pieces,
from the point of view of a four hundred-year-old syphilitic tuna

named Laverne. She told me writers were just actors
too lazy to work restaurant shifts.
We filled the back of the Volvo with strange aquatic monologues
and two sleeping bags that zipped together awkwardly.

We stopped at a Community College just south of the city,
a place suburban kids get diplomas in Hospitality and Tourism

instead of getting jobs so that they could finally move out
of their parents' basements.

We befriended a young couple, Harold and Maude,
(who knew only of Cat Stevens as a terrorist
and had surely just failed Menu Planning exams),
shared American Spirits and weak, warm American beer.

We roamed the Emerald City on streets not of yellow brick,
finding no wizard, but rather a mellowed back alley bar
that served exclusively, seductively and unapologetically,
Loose Corn Daiquiris and Jager.

With each kernelled drink and Green River b-side,
her eyes filled further with tears like fisheye dreams,
knowing today maybe she'd loved the last of me.

Staggering into a vagrant's night,
we walked the maze of dishonest sidewalks,
claiming their loyalty,
and streets named for trees
and sixteenth century explorers,

searching for a '76 Volvo with a cerulean door,
through a park where she said she had lost her virginity,
and bounded into the night as if had she looked hard enough
we might be able to find it in a soft decade's lazy growth.

In a hotel room where Hendrix
once ate oatmeal with a small spoon,
she dreams in Spanish,
whispering truths she wouldn't dare
in waking or English.

Her body recedes into mine.

EUGENE, OREGON
It's a stranger's life on the I-5,
each mile compounds a nagging hatred
for all things imperial.
How many gallons in a day?
Miles in a silence?

Amusement park gas stations
with Urge Overkill logos,
road apple discount bins,
blue smocked attendants
tirelessly awaiting some kind end.

From the jade and olive of Washington
and part of the O in Oregon
she drank pony cans of Bud,
monopolized the stereo
with local college radio stations.

Christian billboards reminded us
of faults not yet attained,
like notions of episodic lives,
like the desire to fuck
each other's closest friends.

She wanted to spend the night in Eugene and visit Ken Kesey.
We didn't make it to Kesey's, because it was late
and he's been dead for seven years.
Instead she sleeps off road apples in a Motel 6.

Ephedrine and caffeine had expected a longer day.
I flipped through the phone book, curious to see
if there was another me living close by.
I had a listing at 1772 Hilyard. I called. I wasn't home,
but had a clever voice mail message and a wife named Marnie.

I wondered where I might be on a Sunday in late October,
maybe in a cheap motel room in Vancouver
calling me and being disappointed,
in my voice mail's sad plea:
"I'll be home soon, please leave a message. Please."

We had breakfast at Denny's
where the waitress seemed unimpressed
by the beauty of my companion's smile,
or to answer my questions about white gravy
and the baseball theme. No Hospitality diploma I supposed.

I wonder if anyone in Eugene
will ever read this and say:
"Hey, I live there; I know that Denny's,
and what the fuck is a Loose Corn Daiquiri?"

HOPE, CALIFORNIA
Dark, and lit only by the moon,
that fleeting ghost,
that unfeeling guest,
that goddamn moon.

She wanted to stop
at the road sign for South Weed,
take a photograph
that would make her laugh

when she was forty,
and had two friends named Diane.
I refused to stop.
I will not like Diane. I will not know Diane.

Years later I'll find a map with its towns out of order,
in some cases improperly named.
Missing is Hope, a truck stop in Northern California

where I'm waiting in a two-tone Volvo wagon
for her to come back with a forty of discount Vodka,
and that smile, that says we may have never been there at all.

II. Battery Milk

Now Accepting Applications for Hotel Reception

It was the year of the vagina embargo
and red was no longer a flavour.

Townsfolk were humbled
when the condoms expired,
though Bill, the proud Irish setter,
seemed indifferent as he tended to be
towards all matters prophylactic or unshiny.

Liquor was illegal and virgins were scarce.
Writers everywhere were committing suicide
with similies, effortlessly and with a flawless grace.
Pictures of Jesus were torn from walls
and replaced with shrines to Donnie Moore.

The women conspired and invested in vibrators,
the men, erect and lonesome, envied batteries.
They turned to tissues and eventually ran out of Kleenex,
they tried fucking each other and empty boxes,
but the love, though poetic, was calloused and unrequited.

In turn they masturbated into warmed banana peels,
convinced themselves of potassium's affection.
Marriage died, the church bells were taken down
and replaced with hollow potatoes. The rains came
and all of the llamas were forced to wear lifejackets,
even the strongest swimmers.

The other livestock voted in favour of monogamy,
the emus abstained and the alpacas snickered.
Vegans celebrated and vegetarians whined.
Pensiones became hotels, syndication was prohibited,
and the left turn was deemed redundant.

They decided against seven, and rallied behind eight.
The constabulary eschewed the moustache and warned
the people of the danger of flowering plants,
promiscuity and postcards. December held April hostage,
and the other months slowly became obsolete.

Bowling trophy wives were replaced
by curling trophy wives. Bill objected
and was shot three times.
Shorts were outlawed except in times of crises,
and cousins were now permitted to play euchre.

They made pancakes upon pancakes
in the shape of ex-lover's diaphragms,
The coast guard was disbanded
and the Portuguese women cried.
Wednesdays would no longer be Wednesdays.
They would, from that moment on, be known as avocadoes.

It was the year of the vagina embargo
and red was no longer a flavour.

More Ponderous than My Tongue

I.
"I could never write a thesis," I said to him
(over a coffee from that village I was in in 2003,
but whose name I forgot in guaro).

"Nothing worth saying is longer than a page."
"Aren't you writing a novel?" he accused,
stirring his chunks of cream,
digging deep to find his sugar,
confused and tired from life in the closet
and a *CSI* marathon on Spike!

"But there's no truth in my novel."
1500 pages of autobiographical bullshit.
Epiphanical grace and tears.
Orosi. That's the name of the village.

II.
She asked what I thought about
the weaponization of space.
I said I opposed all space.

We made passionless abrupt love
and afterwards she told me she believed in God.

I said I opposed all gods,
and yet found him in the fissure
that parted her breasts.

And if she was a good girl,
she'd wipe up what God left
on her sheets.

III.
Someone's nana is going into the fetish shoppe across the street.
She's either getting a substitute lover or change for the number 7.

I try to imagine my own grandmother on public transit.
The thought makes me at once uneasy.

IV.
Dave once told me that happiness is measured
in litres, like milk and backpacks,
but despair is measured in gallons.
I've always admired his simplicity,
and the leisure suit that he only wears on Sundays.

His wife left him last Easter,
a sad and lonely figure
in a corn gallon of polyester.
I guess she loved him more than a carton of 2%,
but less than an MEC daypack.

VI.
That song is playing.
The one where the girl loves the guy,
but he cheats on her,
but she still loves him, and she cries,
but she finds another guy, and he's pure,
and her parents like him too,
even though he's not Episcopalian,
and everything is serendipitous,
and everything works out in three minutes
and twenty-one seconds. You know the one.
The chorus goes: la la la, la la la la, la. La.

1925 Better Not Dance

"And that my friends, is how you fuck a dead cat
with a broomstick." And although I knew Dave
was speaking, as usual, in euphemisms,
it still frightened my grandmother.

This is why we rarely brought
Nana and her cat to the bar, why Dave
was thirty and single, and tangentially
those who weren't liked *According to Jim*.

The room furthered this argument.
Dan sat tucked in Eddie Bauers and sipping Stellas.
Dan had shaved off his long hair at twenty-five,
only to discover he was bald and an asshole.

Dan sits and sips and stares at his Stella's head,
thinks about how he misses head, hair
and the quiet summer of nineteen-ninety.

Outside in the glow, the winners come and go.
And at the end of the bar, flavoured in rye,
the once beautiful says: "1925 better not dance."

"Like a communist squirrel pleasuring six autistic llamas,"
Dave continued, Nana feeling safer.
Two Finger Jimmy moves down the rail
to less euphemistic stools. He coils the bar,

studies his domestic draught, in a white wine glass,
mumbles of easy fisting and a woman named Siobhan,
who smelled like vanilla and semen, who once
Tennessee-waltzed the back alleys of Jimmy's memory,
graceless and unkind, stillborn at forty-five.

Two Fingers fills the jukebox with quarters
and Journey, shares wishful sulphur and easy
wisdom, burns better days and cigarettes
into his unlovèd nub. Jimmy whispers:
"Two Fingers in a smoky room,
a smell of wine and cheap perfume.
For a smile they can share the night,
it goes on and on and on and on."

Nana is sleeping in gin.
Billy Two Shoes models a glass of Grants,
a stained Canadiens tee, and a disdain for all.
"Fucking woman was so boring she made
a coffee filter look like a Rubik's Cube.

My newborn this and my baby that.
Jesus Christ in a new pair of silk boxers
hanging from a ficus lady. If I get drunk
enough I too have unprotected sex,
I just fucking brag about it nine months later."

Two Shoes preaches from a book written in caramel
liquors, by sad adulterers, on pulp and parchment
passed down through our fathers, from a pulpit
so poorly built, its cedar binding under
the weight of dregs and draught and absence.

Outside in the glow, the winners come and go.
And at the end of the bar, flavoured in rye,
the once beautiful says: "1925 better not dance."

The night continues to fight the morning.
But there are hours to fill, there are drinks to be spilled,
spirals to coddle slowly downwards, and to the left.

Dave has heard the name of the Lord, Fingers
has asked Two Shoes if he does not fear trial
for blasphemy. "I don't fear the Lord," says
Two Shoes, "I fear cancer, ex-wives, dimes
and Barbara Frum, just not necessarily in that order."

Dave sticks a straw between Nana's sinking
cheeks and her glass, finishes off her gin and says:
"That's not blasphemy, it ain't even defamation."
A smoke and a smile and in a sigh he proceeds
to show us exactly how one does blaspheme:
"Blasphemer in a smoky room,
a smell of wine and cheap perfume.
For a smile they can share the night,
it goes on and on and on and on."

"I think Eve, if she wasn't so concerned with fruit,
would have fucked off with the snake."
And Dave sinks back to his stool, to another
story, and another night. The hectoring,
as its preachers, will settle, the staggering
sidewalks will lead them all home, waltzing
back alleys in search of one last audience,
or one more drink, or one less beautiful.

Outside in the glow, the winners come and go.
And at the end of the bar, flavoured in rye,
the once beautiful says: "1925 better not dance."

A Christmas Sestina

Nana, that horrible old bitch, is drowned in scotch number four,
smoking two cigarettes and telling me how it is. Crazy bird.
She exhales, billows of smoke filter through her moustache,
up through her snow-white hair. She's Christmas drunk, railing
against Jesus. "Nothing but a hippie nailed to a cross," she says.
I wonder if I can stuff her ninety-eight pound frame into the fire.

The cat slowly urinates into a bowl of chestnuts by the fire.
She's been surly and suffocating since 1984,
just like Nana. Each time a gift is opened, some uncle says
"It's a puppy," to carols of groans. An aunt is having a bird
because my brother's banging my cousin's head into the railing.
After a few hours, oh how that kid's head must ache.

Some illegitimate offspring is enthralled by Nana's moustache,
pulling at it as she dozes. I offer him some matches, hoping fire
will give him devious thoughts. My brother leaves his railing
duties to help and they're able to singe a bit of lip hair before
she awakens. "Put on 'White Christmas'," yells the old bird.
Papa chases his eggnog. "Bing Crosby is an asshole," he says.

Mum appears from the kitchen. "Dinner in ten," she says,
Her nose asks: "What's that odour?" "It's burning moustache,
Mum." I whisper, as I go to the oven to have a peek at our bird.
While she loudly punishes potatoes I go for more firewood,
interrupting Dad and his brother's wife on the deck fornicating.
A hot toddy and mistletoe in hand, she falls over the railing,

a fat angel in the snow. My cousin's been out in his truck railing
coke and fixing his hair. "If it ain't a fuckin' Ford," he says
"you might as well drive a sled. Shit, I bet Santa got a Ford
these days. Big F-350." I tell him there's snow in his moustache.
He picks at the flakes and rubs them into his gums, their fire
numbing his little remaining sense. "Let's kill that bird,"

he exclaims, and I hope he means Nana. But no, 'tis the bird
Mum's been sharing chardonnay with, halfway off the rails,
swearing next year we're going to Florida. The Christmas fire
has withered. "Not nearly enough to burn a body," my Dad says
knowingly, as he licks his festive fingers and parts his moustache.
"Better be good." Mum throws the electric knife at him. Fore.

The moustachioed attack the bird. It takes me
four tries to free the cousin from the railing guillotine.
My brother says nothing as he tosses our presents into the fire.

Brandon, Population: 41 511

It was January 4th, 2007,
and I could no longer distinguish nightmares from Thursdays.
I had thought admitting to putting pinholes in the condoms
would make you laugh. Instead you threw a lamp.

We could have lived in Montreal, I think, celebrated
unprotected sex with baby showers and diamonds,
instead of the morning after pill and Gravol.
You and morphine would have had a beautiful child. Opietta.

I had suggested Brandon, but you said Ontario
was no place to be married or alone, no place to raise a child.
And Brandon is in Manitoba, but that didn't seem to matter.

Nor did it matter you no longer drank milk,
John Ritter was dead and was very much unlikely to return,
or how I always spelled February with one 'r'.

Or that I believed people would watch TV again,
if they just took the Bibles out of hotel rooms,
if criminal forensics would become just a little less popular.

If unrequited became a verb, like when I lived out west
and I unrequited the shit out of my girlfriend,
until she left me for the guy across the hall who played guitar,
well known to lonely girls for never unrequiting.

When you left you took the litter box, but left the cat,
declaring platonic to be pedestrian, promising reunion.
Three years later and the Mile End is gentrified, but still lonely.

I heard that you had a friend take you to the clinic
and that you celebrated with cosmos at some lounge on The Main.
Heard you got that job in Toronto, that you're happy there,
that you call home T Dot, and you don't hate yourself for it.

And I heard you met your husband at a function at the Drake.
He told you he loved his girlfriend, but she was often in Ottawa,
and you were on your last drink. And you are pregnant (again).

And Brandon has grown considerably in recent years
and is now comparable in size to other midsize cities
such as Newmarket, St. Catherines, and Belleville.

Skate Betty

My son has just come into the room. He's four.
He's wearing his winter boots on the wrong feet
and carrying a photograph of you found in the basement.

I. I Started Something I Couldn't Finish
I'd come pick you up, stoned and hopeful,
from you parents place on Crossfield,
that last block always taken so slowly,
terrified of your father.

He would stare at me knowingly,
sip from his glass of Dewar's,
flip through his Stihl catalogue,
fondle images of power tools,
as we waited for you to come downstairs.

Sometimes he would fix me a drink,
though I was too young to drink,
certainly too young to drink with your father.
And he would look at me,
with the scotch shaking in my hand,
whisper across the room your mother
decorated in Robert Bateman paintings:
"Son, if you try and put that sorry little excuse
for a cock inside of my daughter, I'll fucking cut it off,
put it with my fishing gear and use it as tackle."
Although I'm sure he meant bait.
To which I'd reply: "Sir, you know as well as I do
that your fine young daughter does not like cock.
She eschews the cock. In fact sir, she likes pussy
much like, I assume, you do."

But I'd say it all with my eyes,
sip my drink quietly, cross my legs,
think about Red Devil lures
and angry routers.

II. Girlfriend in a Coma
I was too young to be a beard,
too young to grow a beard.
You and I would walk to Sara's house,
I'd be hoping all the while that on the way
you'd get hit by a car, fall into a coma,
and wake up three months later straight,
and maybe in love with me.

I'd sit in Sara's parents' basement
sucking down BT's from a weathered
plastic diet Pepsi bottle, exhaling through
a toilet paper roll stuffed with Downy,
listening to Sara's collection
of fashionable British indie,
while the two of you giggled
behind the door of the adjacent guest room.
To this day I hate The Smiths,
I feel nauseous around laundry rooms.

Sometimes you'd come join me, briefly,
roll a little joint and let me kiss you
so I could know what Sara tasted like,
what you tasted like.

III. Is It Really So Strange?
My mum would often ask about you.
"Where's your little girlfriend?"
    "She's not my girlfriend, Mum."
"Why isn't she your girlfriend?"
    "Because she has a girlfriend, Mum."
"Well that's just silly."
And then she'd bake oatmeal chocolate chip cookies,
    contented and heavy on the Crisco.

My father would often ask about you.
"Where's your sweet little girlfriend?"
    "She's not my girlfriend, Dad."
"Why isn't she your girlfriend?"
    "Because she has a girlfriend, Dad."
"Does she have a sister?"
And then he'd find his smokes and his Lay-Z-Boy,
    disappointed and light on advice.

IV. Hand in Glove
You told me I could tell my friends we were fucking.
 I told my friends we were in love,
with uninformed embellishment,
because the only things I had fucked
were my right hand, a few decorative throw cushions,
and a Harrods' tea cozy.

And my right hand, my mum's good throw cushions
and a souvenir from London
did not do the wonderful things
I told my friends we had done.
Cushions could not bend that way.
The cozy cursed with but one orifice,
and was a selfish lover and ignorant partner.
And my right hand was always in a hurry,
worried my mother would come barging into the bathroom
raging about what the dog had done to her cushions.

V. This Night Has Opened My Eyes
On New Year's Eve 1992
Sara's parents had gone to New York.
The three of us celebrated in her basement,
drank Baby Duck and Laurentide
did shots of my dad's pilfered Captain Morgan's
danced to Morrissey, cursed Johnny Marr.
At midnight the two of you kissed
and wouldn't stop.
You pulled me into the guest room,
said I could watch, or whatever.
I was too nervous to masturbate, or whatever.
Though I would recall the images
countless times in the years that followed.

The two of you were nothing like
the *Bleu Nuit* movies on Channel 5
that interrupted so many *Saturday Night Lives*.
I was left with a few lingering questions:
Like why did they call it donut bumping?
Did it ever feel like you were loving a malleable mirror?
Why hadn't the subject been covered in Health Ed?
I left before you were finished,
believing afterglow was not something to be observed.

It snowed that night. Living rooms were aglow
in "Auld Lang Syne" and midnight couples.
My solitary tracks marked the virginal snow,
trudged a weaving path across the park to home.

VI. Louder Than Bombs
When Sara started dating Sean Miller, you were crushed.
You spent a week locked in your room
crying and listening to "How Soon is Now?".
Your folks thought it was my fault,
your dad called my dad,
and empty scotch laced threats were exchanged.
The Stihl catalogue was referenced
and it was apparent that my dad's life
and Honda Civic were in peril.

Your mum spread horrible rumours
about my brother Paul's sexuality
and my mum's Chardonnay afternoons,
throughout the neighbourhood.
Paul became reclusive and Mum found herself banned
from book clubs from Hawkesbury to Smiths Falls.

My mum asked: "What happened between you and your little girlfriend?"
    "She's not my girlfriend Mum."
"Well not anymore she isn't."
    "She got dumped by her girlfriend Mum."
"Well that's just silly."
And she sat down to discuss *The Pelican Brief* with Paul,
    with lukewarm tea and opinions of John Grisham.

My dad asked: "What happened between you and your sweet little girlfriend?"
    "She's not my girlfriend Dad."
"Couldn't make her come could you?"
    "She got dumped by her girlfriend Dad."
"You should get on that while it's vulnerable."
And then we sat down to discuss the myth of the female orgasm,
    one eye on the driveway and unimpressed by Alex Comfort.

VII. Hatful of Hollow
Late August, 1993.
My parents had gone to Merrickville
to a little boutique that made custom cushions,
and Paul had gone out for coffee
and two copies of *The Client*.
You showed up on my back porch
with a bottle of your mum's Bombay.
We mixed it with cranberry juice,
sat on my bed in silence.
Sara was going to Queen's the next week with Sean
to study Art History, and join a sorority.

You kissed me and I shivered.
Your eyes, brown pools of warm promise.
Your touch, numb and frightening.

You guided me gently inside of you,
and I swear you were crying,
but your eyes would not find mine.

VIII. All You Need is Me
I found out at your funeral that you were pregnant.
Your dad took me aside, ushered me to the basement.

We drank Dewar's from the flask you had bought him
on a class trip to Quebec City in grade 8.

He told me. He told me you were six weeks.
He told me he found you in the backyard,

hanging from an Oak tree we never carved our initials into.
He told me he loved you, and he knew, and he cried,

and we got drunk while the well-wishers
exchanged pleasantries and false goodwill,

while young men shuffled in their fathers' suits,
while Sara chose an outfit in which to attend convocation,

and summer passed on and fall didn't care,
nor winter, nor spring, and so on, and so on.

IX. There Is A Light that Never Goes Out
My son has just come into the room. He's four.
He's wearing his winter boots on the wrong feet
and carrying a photograph of you found in the basement.

My son asks: "Was this your girlfriend Dad?"
　"She was not my girlfriend."
'Why wasn't she your girlfriend Dad?"
　"Because she had a girlfriend."
"That's silly."
And he sits on my lap and traces your figure in the photograph,
and I will take him fishing next spring,
and he'll get older and make mistakes,
and one day, when he's eight, we'll run into your dad
in the parking lot at Home Depot,
and I'll introduce them,
and on the ride home my son may ask
why that nice man looked so sad.

III. Convenience

Charity

I.
I wake up at four-eleven every morning,
not out of duty or responsibility,
but to see if you're still breathing
though I know you're not there.

I had a dream recently in which I wore fur,
had a love affair with a hamster named Siobhan.
I felt guilty for weeks, made a donation I couldn't afford to PETA
and slept with the comely Irish girl who works

at the Starbucks across from your office.
When I kissed her I opened my eyes,
was startled by your absence,
the scar on your cheek erased.

By four-eleven she was gone.
I immediately changed the sheets.

II.
On Tuesdays I smoke Matinee menthols on Mount Royal.
They taste clean and I hope they'll have that effect.
I worry about cancer, though relish the thought of attention.
Like you bringing me a new Trilby

for my chemo-balding head,
or renting me *10 Things I Hate About You*,
so we can continue to despise Julia Stiles,
and secretly begin to devise our own lists.

I hate the way you use the word 'friend' like a weapon.
I hate the way you touch me when you're sober.
I hate the way you're always fucking other men.
I hate the way you expect me to love you and no other.

I make an online donation to the Canadian Cancer Society,
and switch back to Peter Jacksons for the rest of the week.

III.
I worry about the trees I've killed with superfluous rhymes
and using the word soul without really knowing what it means.
*Darling, you're my soulmate, we've invested in soulfate,
we're so deeply in soullove, like soulflowers and souldoves.*

Last week I got a rejection letter from McSweeney's.
It read: "The rainforests called; they said they're depleting."
It was a short story in which Jesus is resurrected
but nobody notices. He marries a girl from Thunder Bay,

opens a succesful Greek restaurant and they have three sons
who shun the responsibility of messiahdom and souvlaki.
Instead they have aspirations to play in the NHL,
save the youngest who wants to be a dancer.

Jesus disowns him out of fear that the child's love
for jazz tap means he's gay, which of course it does.

IV.
Again I realize I have trouble separating
speaker and self, feel guilty for my blasphemy
even though I've recently converted to Judaism
because Jesus is just some guy with good tzatziki

and problems with progeny, living up
the Bay. I make humble donations
to the Catholic League, the B'nai Brith
and Jews for Jesus. Just to be sure.

I masturbate. Last night I was fantasizing
about white walls and Third World child labour,
trying to deter myself delay gratification
so that my right hand could come first.

Neither of us did and I'm immediately reminded
of our third anniversary and all of my unlovèd emissions.

V.
This morning I donated my last three hundred dollars
to Planned Parenthood, burned my Nikes and Gap t-shirts,
drew your silhouette from memory on my bedroom wall,
made a noose out of my fitted sheet
with no intention of putting it to use,
but rather to understand the intricate complication of the knot.
After all, it's four-eleven and I have nothing else to do.

The Convenience of Jack

I've been spending sleepless mornings
exploring the convenience of blackouts,
the intricate patterns in smoke stained ceilings,
the sounds my walls make.

I've got an engagement ring in a forgotten drawer,
with stacks of half-written poems
and cocktail napkin knowledge,
expiring condoms keeping celibacy safe,
a half bottle of gin, lipstick stained and desperate for tonic.

I've spoken of Jack before. Jack haunts me.
Jack is my cancer, my curse, my enemy,
my competition, my solace, my sanity.
Jack is the anti-Christ, an antiquated empty loathing.
Jack is born of my jealous nature, of my unsteady hands.
Jack drinks what I spill.

It should be noted here, I have never met Jack.
I have seen him, though, in pictures mostly,
in midday nightmares, in epiphanies lost in drink,
clouds of calming that disappear in the discomfort of sobriety.

Jack, I'd have to assume, played lacrosse in university,
because I fucking hate lacrosse. Or anything to do with wickets.
Cricket, banks, croquet. Ewoks.
Jack majored in Business Admin or Commerce.
One of those degrees that gets you a career as a financial planner,
affairs with secretaries in pleated power suits
who claim to be "executive administrative assistants,"
a loft followed by a condo followed by a townhouse
followed by a suburban four bedroom followed by a divorce.
Jack's friends are all from university,
they call each other by their last names,

they hosted keg parties in houses
three cockroaches shy of being condemned,
brought their laundry home to their mothers on weekends.
They exchanged girlfriends so often
they might as well have shared a penis.
And they were cruel to that penis,
putting it in places more awful than Kirsten Dunst,
putting it in sad girls happy for frat boy attention,
putting it on occasion in one another,
though they'll never admit it.
Jack and his friends drank draught beer,
though they all secretly despised it,
and when left alone in the quiet cocksure corners of sports bars
they'd drink rye and gingers, quickly, shamefully, sadly.

Jack fucks my wife.
Jack is fucking my wife right now.
Jack is pulling her hair,
whispering suggestions of loveless deviance,
marking her freckled velvet petal skin with angry scrapes,
of avaricious well manicured nails.
Jack is inside my wife, unprotected, uncaring,
screaming out his low round, his net worth,
his credit card limit, his address.
Jack asks about me.
Jack compares himself as he comes.
Jack laughs my name as he lights my wife's cigarette,
caresses her hair, breathes in her scent.

I have recurring dreams, in which Jack kicks my ass.
I never was one for sports, and I lack Jack's build.
Jack hits me with a bottle, sometimes a bottle of 50,
sometimes imported Italian balsamic, which stings even in sleep.
Jack cuts me for eleven stitches. Always eleven.
Jack steals my Health card as I writhe in pain, just to be a prick.
This is so fucking Jack. These are my dreams.

In my nightmares, I kick the shit out of Jack.
In my nightmares I have played intramural soccer,
and have an upper body that doesn't remind lovers
of Don Knotts – Don Knotts in the Mr. Furley years.
But I feel guilty, and I rush Jack to the emergency room,
buy him an overpriced hospital concession Diet Peach Snapple
as he sits in a wicket, motherfucking wickets,
and hands over his unpilferred Health card,
tells me about how wet my wife gets,
about his new Callaway driver,
about victory, and how it tastes not unlike tamarind.

Jack will father my children. Jack will own my house.
Jack will leer at my sister-in-law at Christmas dinner.
Jack will compliment my wife's dry turkey.
Jack will pass off CNN opinion as his own.
Jack will steal jokes and fuck up the punch line.
Six midgets in the trunk of a Volkswagen. Get it?
Jack will pepper conversations with "top shelf".
Jack will name my dog Jack out of ego,
and a simple sense of humour.
Jack will always smell faintly
like the men's cosmetic counter at the Bay.
Jack will pass by me, unknowingly, on bending sidewalks,
in crowded bars, in jaded lanes of fading memories.
Jack will never, not fucking once,
shiver when my wife enters the room.

Jane (Montreal)

Tomorrow is September,
and I'm going to miss August
the way I miss your dad.

And on a rain tired day like today,
when outside is a memory of Vancouver,
but inside is all Montreal,

where no song seems to suit,
and only stale cigarettes and cold coffee
make the afternoon tolerable.

Well, it's on days like these
that I wonder where you are,
even as I know where you are,

if you're wearing those socks
you took from me last April,
and never returned.

Because they mean more to you,
than they ever could to me,
because they're just wool socks

in desperate need of darning.
And as I wait for the grey to mellow into night,
I agonize about whether or not

your tea has steeped to your liking.
Just this side of bitter,
and a lifetime away from me

Harrison Ford, Perhaps

You still have a key to the apartment,
sometimes I wonder if you come by,
when I'm at work. Wrap yourself in my sheets,
try to find us in the memory of my pillows.

I know you don't. You're in other apartments now,
a condo maybe. Something by the Lachine Canal,
bought by some asshole you tolerate,
for convenience, comfort, and the joy of a small cock.

Thoughts of this cock, the condo, that cock,
keep me awake. I have tried drinking myself
to sleep, but the scent and sight of empty
bottles reminds me of you.

I've tired of taking Ativan,
purchased from homeless men,
pestering a drunken terrace,
for just five dollars of forgiveness.

It turned out to be Adderall,
wrestled me further in wake.
Eyes burring gin-scented silences,
washing solutions away in sleeplessness.

I've tired of masturbating,
and I can no longer think of you when I do.
I mean, I can, but it's not helpful.
Futile familiarity lacks the sweet contrivance

that my right hand so richly deserves, working in reverse.
You begin naked, dress quickly, talk about your feelings,
about notions of dissolving faith,
about famous carpenters other than Jesus.

I've tired of fantasy, Lindsay Lohan and her ample
décolletage, it seems to work. But LiLo, bless her heart,
naked as the day is ridiculous, has problems,
problems that I try to fix in fantasy,

as I tried to fix in you. In this sleep deprived whimsy
Lindsay is taking cabs, doing less blow, fucking good men,
choosing better scripts and better company.
There's talk of a *Herbie* sequel.

The wake leaves me idle and confused.
Enjoying a smoke on my stoop, and admiring a pigeon,
I immediately thought: "Hey, nice cat."

Confused, like when I walk by an open window
in the Plateau and hear a familiar song, I think:
"Hey, maybe I live here now."

Confused, like when someone says eleven,
someone else says tabarfuck, and yet another says Dexadrine,
and the beginning of the conversation is lost forever.

Confused, like when contrivance and fantasy fail,
sleep is but a memory of better hours, and a naked
and needing starlet or ex-lover can't deliver
happier endings or restful nights.

3 1/2

I.
A row of apartments better that mine rival cable
for a poor man's attentions. I have no cable,
just wishful rabbit ears pulling faint signals from a cluttered sky.

Today there is nothing on, except for the gay couple
third window from the left,
second floor, who seem to be arguing.
They finish in tears, with one guy storming out.

Two weeks later I will serve him at the bar
as he gently fondles a young girl I think I once knew.
They tip me poorly and I side with his spurned lover.

II.
A gentle rain and feverish construction scrambles all reception.
Books I have never read once again fail
to grasp my attention.

A small joint from last night's ashes provokes me
to do the dishes, yet halfway through I am distracted
by a nest of silverfish I spot between the fridge and the stove.
I spend the remainder of the afternoon taking photographs
I will never develop and believing myself to be an artist.

III.
The girl in the apartment across the way,
second from the right, top floor,
is naked and crying again.

For a moment I think I'm in love with her,
but it turns out I've just watched too many sitcoms.
I imagine myself the lead,

etching my phone number into the glass
as in some shampoo commercial.
She notices the number and calls immediately.

We meet at a bistro that reminds me of place I've never been.
We both are huge Will Oldham fans and make plans
to see him soon, together, somewhere.

After dinner we take a long walk around Mount Royal.
When we tire, we find a secluded spot
in the comfort of a late summer's growth
where we make love as joggers and rapists pass us,
happily, unknowingly.

I walk her home, right to the door like a gentleman.
I give her soft cheek a taste and we decide to meet for breakfast.
She never calls.
The next week a small ruddy man with a Chesapeake retriever
moves in with her. How cruel:
a big dog like that with no yard to run in.

IV.
My neighbours below are fucking like angry rabbits,
an odd soundtrack for the couple directly across the way
who I have been watching trying to tango for almost three hours.
I admire the stamina of all four.

V.
Today I turn thirtyish and celebrate
with more cocaine than I need.
My coffee table is like a dark highway
slowly losing its lines under the speed of my will
to drive faster than I did at twentyish.
And suddenly I feel very strange.
And suddenly my teeth feel like battery milk.
And suddenly tomorrow feels a little bit closer.
And suddenly I begin to think that you tried.

I decide to go for a walk knowing that the coke
will keep me up well into tomorrow anyway.
Find myself on a dock on the Lachine Canal,
knee deep in the brown water, my shoes nowhere to be found.
They're my only pair.

I can feel the sun rising behind me
and a slow city rising with it.
I trudge home barefoot arriving an hour later,
feet bloodied and a mouthful of chalk.

I resolve not to do coke again until I'm twentyish again,
and to own at least two pairs of shoes for the rest of my days.
I will be unsuccessful on both counts.

VI.
The unexpected October heat woke me,
but it was the fire engines that got me out of bed.

Across the way my theatre was burning.
All of my characters spilled out on to the street
as their homes crumbled like excuses,
singed their crying eyes.

The Chesapeake retriever snarled.
The spurned lover,
the tired tangoists,
the big dog's undeserving owner,
became viewers, like me.

The following weeks were filled
with the smell of damp smoke
and afternoons of *Coronation Street*.
I covered the windows with dark curtains.

Coming home from work one day I struck up a conversation
with one of the construction guys.
He told me there had been an insurance problem
The lot would likely remain vacant for years
as the parties fought through civil court.

At night I sneak onto the charred lot
and dance a lonely tango
to the echoing familiarity
of voices I'd never heard.

A Rented Suit

I.
I've been hiding in a house of half-emptied beer cans,
occasionally paying a prostitute to be my mentor
and therapist, admitting to her, in a moment of weakness,
I like oranges but I am entirely indifferent about the apple.

She's told me to concentrate more
on my assonance and allegories,
but I've been horribly busy
with empty bottles and punch lines.

What did the half-bottle of whiskey say to the half-bottle of gin?
"You'll never know raw passion until you've slithered
 between Anne Murray's soft and wanting thighs."

What did the orange say to the apple?
"For a deaf/mute quadriplegic, you can sure sing."

What did the drunk unshaven fuck in the rented suit say to Jane?
"I've come to get my girl and take her home."

II.
Jack said it was time we met, time we put down or swords,
time we stopped measuring cocks and just admitted he is bigger.
We met in the bar your cousin once owned,
the bar where I first lied to you, the bar where I proposed,
but the proposition came out in the ghost of a broken whisper.

Jack said he was not my competition,
and it was time to admit my defeat.
Jack didn't know I had put aside my intentions,
resolved my differences with citrus, or that
the hooker charges fifty dollars for sex,

but five hundred for written comments.
Jack paid the bill, laughed at inside my head,
his stare lingered longingly on the waitress' ass.

I should not have been invited to the wedding
but Jane, you always loved theatre.
I should not have drank a bottle of Stolly
with your brother before the service.

I should not have been invited to the wedding.
I should not have made a toast,
and that toast should not have included:
"I miss the way your scent lingers a room,
the way you dance when you're nervous,
the way your taste would rest on my tongue for days,
the way you'd scream 'dead monkey bubble' as you came.
The way my memory writes you."
I should not have been invited to the wedding.

Your father was very delicate in administering my beating,
only eleven stitches, but I had to pay Moore's for the suit.
He drove me to the hospital, did you know that?
Told me Jack was a prick and a 'bit of a fag',
but Jack was beautiful, he had money and your hand,
and I had a fractured orbital bone and little else.

If I had just liquidated the open bar
and fucked a bridesmaid.
If I had grown a beard, teased the morning
with the possibility of sleep.
If I had told you I loved you,
instead of loving the emptying bottle.

Your thank you card was humourless and formulaic.
Dear you, thanks for the whatever.
Jack left a message on my voice mail,

thanking me for breaking you in and for a lovely toaster oven.

III.
I'm a dishonest and selfish lover,
the mullet is making a comeback,
and I should have declined the invitation.

    My prostitute says I'm kind and loyal,
    that I please her, though I pay her,
    and accepting the invitation made her proud.

I mix my metaphors, I'm greying prematurely,
my characters are stock and unripened
and I should get checked for Chlamydia.

    My prostitute says I mix a good drink,
    my grey hair makes me look wise and handsome,
    and that no one really gets Chlamydia anymore.

I suffer from a jealous nature,
a quick release and abandonment issues,
and whomever I fuck, I only see one face.

    My prostitute says my jealousy is protective,
    that when the lights go out we're all abandoned,
    and if I want to keep calling her Jane, that's okay.

Dear Jane,

I'm sitting on the terrace at a pub in the Annex in Toronto. I tell people I'm here visiting friends, but I don't know why I'm here. Occasionally I look up to see if you might walk by, even though I know you're a five-day walk from me. They say I should stop loving you, but they say a lot of things. What are they telling you?

I wanted to write you a love letter,
until I was told people don't do that anymore,
like making mixed tapes and cutting
covers from pictures out of magazines,
or washing your hands after pissing.

I'm thirty-two now, but I guess you'd know that. My hair is greyed. I live in one of those apartments in Mile End that smell like Arcade Fire but is supposed to increase my artist caché. Some band lives below me. They play a lot of Silver Jews covers, and I often find myself spending nights alone drinking, one ear pressed to the hardwood, trying to find you in the lyrics. I wear a lot of band T-shirts. I prefer Starbucks to Tim Hortons, though I'm a little ashamed of it. I still tend bar at that place. My dad died. I drink too much.

My letter suffered from a lack of will.
It diffused into a rambling narrative,
complete with thinly veiled pseudonyms,
evidence of a fractured voice
that surely isn't mine.

How you love Cheerios,
but are terrified of their symmetry.
And I came up with the whole symmetry thing
(by the by) long before you quizzed me

on my views on symmetry and asymmetry
and abortion. Just a cosmic coincidence I guess,
something you don't seem to believe in
or blissfully ignore.

*There's things you may not know about me, Jane. I was born
forty-two minutes after I wanted to be, in a building adjacent to
the Grace Army General, by a midwife to a disinterested and
drug-free mother, everybody singing "Down by the River" to
ease mother's pain and fray my mind. Don't shoot me. Or take
me seriously.*

My friend Jena told me to "buck up,"
like people really say "buck up" anymore
and maybe never did, but swear on the Bible
she said buck up and that everyone has obstacles,
like Jena's husband is a francophone
from New Brunswick
but she's been able to work past it.

She also recommended I leave out
some of the incidental details of my former life
like my propensity towards jealousy,
or my arrest while living in Virginia in 1998
for stalking a four-year-old colt.
I said colt, in case you misheard.

*I tell you these things, Jane, because I don't think you believe
that I'm real. It's getting up I have issues with. You've said you
love me, but I'm beginning to believe you use the word 'love' as a
synonym for 'know'. Did you know that after you left, I drank
for three straight weeks? Woke up in the arms of your enemy,
convinced that her tangled anger could fix me. It didn't, and now
she's late.*

I've left the letter for a few hours now,
and come back to it after a few drinks now.
And I'm eating an overcooked Virginia ham
(goddamn puritan fucking Virginia,
and its sweet sweet equine talent).

And I'm eating this ham with my grandfather's spork,
and a Swiss Army Knife missing its nail file,
and I consider why the spork isn't more popular,
and while inspecting my cuticles I wonder aloud,
in a poorly constructed slur, if this is the part of me
you love or don't, maybe.
Or is it the part of me that wears sunglasses
in funeral homes and plays catch with stray dogs.

I only ask because earlier I was talking
to a terrier lab mutt who believed strongly
(though with great bias) that it's the latter
and a chihuahua beagle (fittingly named Jack)
trusts in the former, though admits
that he may be woefully misinformed,

and a schnauzer retriever
with a weak little girl's bladder
who had ditched his owner
in High Park believes somewhat convincingly
that you don't even like me.

A pair of your jeans still hang, unwashed, on the back of my bathroom door. Your cowboy boots are still in the front hallway, my Palace Brothers T-shirt tucked into the left one. You had promised to wash it. I'm afraid to move it, as if it can hold our place in time. Every note, every card, every letter you ever wrote me are stuffed into my grandfather's silver cigarette case in my living room. I find a living room, parenthetically, poorly titled.

Which brings me back to you,
and your sweet doe eyes.
The way your voice is an octave higher
in bed or when you're apologetic.

Your tightened grip during feline nightmares.
Your head resting beneath my chin when you're pensive.
The smile you get when I catch you looking my way.
The way you hold my hand when I'm driving.
The way I can map our past by the scars on your cheek.
The sound my name makes when it rolls off your tongue.
The story of the night we met.
The memory of the first time I saw you.
The slight husk in your tempered voice.
How you're shy when you curse.
How you have to qualify the word "love".
How you hate your mother, but call her anyway.
How technology and syndication confuse you.
The sweet flavour of your left nipple.
The feeling of my mouth on the back of your neck.
The subtle curve of your inner thigh.
How I still shiver when you enter a room.

The way every time we say goodbye,
I quietly wish you a good life.

I'm washing the dishes. Some cups are still lipstick stained. The drain still clogs during the summers, for some reason. I have too many glasses, though I've taken to drinking exclusively from your travel mug. I like to keep the place tidy now. It's always quiet. I go days without speaking. Tonight I'll go down to Mount Royal Park, sit in the fading sun as the summer goes by, pretend to read a book. I'll take off my glasses, and feel the warm nervous flutter of believing that every girl who walks past, is you.

Acknowledgements

Line 15 in "Rented Suit I" is from "Tennessee" by the Silver Jews, written by David Berman © 2001 Civil Jar Music.

Earlier versions of the following poems have appeared elsewhere, for which I wish to thank the editors. " The Convenience of Jack" (*Matrix* no. 79), "Now Accepting Applications for Hotel Reception" and "Calculated Distractions in the Absence of Someone Named Jane" (*Pistol*, PistolPress, 2008), "Charity and Ampersand" (*Headlight Anthology* 10) and "More Ponderous Than My Tongue" (*Soliloquies* 9). Additionally the Loose Corn Daiquiri was invented by Toby Hughes.

Thank you, first of all, to my editor, Dave McGimpsey. His friendship, mentorship, honesty, and patient guidance have done more for my writing than I could ever articulate.

Thanks to Jon Paul Fiorentino at *Matrix* magazine and Snare Books for believing in this book, and for being an invaluable friend.

Thanks to my many profs who layed the foundation for this book in various stages, particularily Stephanie Bolster, Mikhail Iossel, Padgett Powell, and Jason Camlot.

Thanks to Marisa Grizenko for being an amazing copyeditor.

Many, many thanks to the friends who have supported me in various ways as this book was being written; Greg Seib, Joe and Krista Gerard, Brian Davis, Nathalie Edwards-Leroux, Devon Saurette, Jena Menchetti, Jean-Phillipe Bourgeois, and Innis Mccourty.

To Dave Baker, whose virtue and friendship is boundless and inspirational, thanks for always answering the phone, no matter the hour.

A very special thanks goes to Nick McArthur and Hillary Rexe, who edited and added to these poems with skill and honesty before anyone had ever seen them, and quite often before they were written.

But, above all things and all people, thanks to my family. To my sister Ainsley Spry, for being endlessly honest. To my brother-in-law Redmond Weissenberger for bringing a unique and loving voice into our family. To my niece and nephew, Piper and Finn Weissenberger, for unknowingly keeping me grounded and sane during the final days of editing. And to my amazing parents, Toby and Andrea Spry, whose undying love and support has allowed me the space to make many mistakes, and given me the time to try and fix them.